FIRE HOUSE ANTICS

By

Charles L. Bose

This book is a work of non-fiction. Names and places have been changed to protect the privacy of all individuals. The events and situations are true.

© 2003 by Charles L. Bose. All rights reserved.

No part of this book may be reproduced, stored in a retrieval system, or transmitted by any means, electronic, mechanical, photocopying, recording, or otherwise, without written permission from the author.

ISBN: 1-4140-0902-X (e-book)
ISBN: 1-4140-0901-1 (Paperback)
ISBN: 1-4140-0900-3 (Dust Jacket)

This book is printed on acid free paper.

1stBooks - rev. 10/24/03

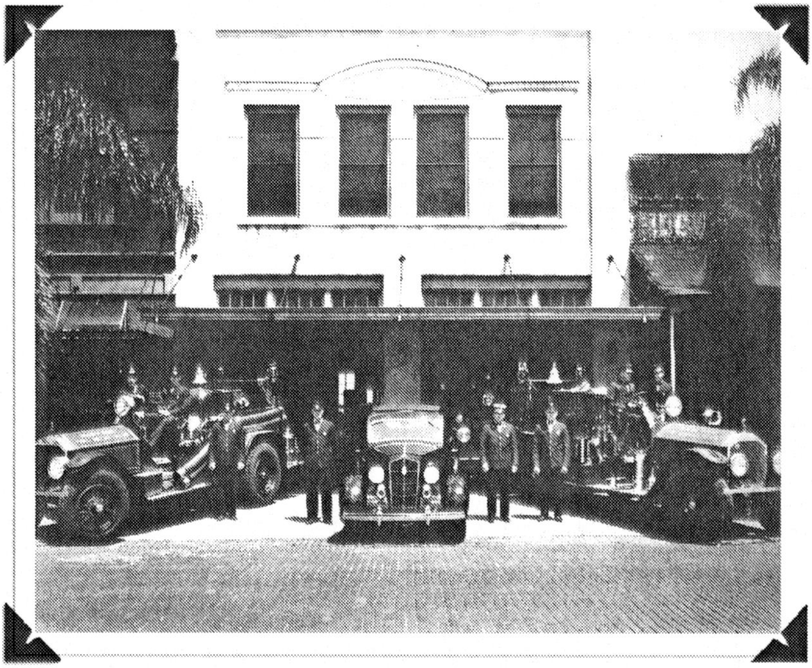

Dedication

To all my firefighting brother and sisters … living and deceased; and to my wife and family … for their worrying during the time I was on duty protecting the lives and property of the citizens of Sanford.

Foreword

I have been retired now for thirteen years and I would still rather fight a fire than eat supper. It seems that once a firefighter always one.

I remember during the 9-11 terrorist attack I was returning from vacation in Ohio when I heard the news of the attack on the Twin Towers in New York City. I was on I-77 just about to the West Virginia line. I told my wife, "I feel like turning around and going to New York where I can be with my 'brother' firefighters to help them at this terrible time." But due to health and distance I figured I'd be better off if I stayed home and prayed for them and supported their efforts in other ways.

I wrote a song in tribute to the New York Fire Department. It is called *The Firefighters*. I included it in a CD with sixteen other songs that we (a group called "Cabin Companions") wrote and produced. The words to the song are included in this book on the last page.

In Sanford the retired firefighters gather at the fire station one day a month and one of the retired firefighters always cooks a meal for lunch. It is a time when all the stories are retold and the active firefighters get a chance to sit, eat and interact with us, the retired firemen. The honor is ours to pass on old tricks, etc. to the younger firefighters.

Author's Notes

This book is not divided into chapters, but into stories. Some are short; some are longer; all are of actual events that happened during my time on duty. Some stories are very difficult to impart; in fact, they have been almost impossible.

Preface

This book is about my experiences, funny and tragic, during my twenty-five years as a firefighter. Let me give you some background information before I begin.

The town I write about is Sanford, Florida. At my hiring it was a town of approximately 17,000 in population, located 5 miles south of Interstate 4, between Daytona and Orlando. Sanford was a quiet town; many called it a bedroom community of Orlando. Most people from Orlando either did not know or care where Sanford was.

For one reason or another we had one of the best and probably the oldest fire departments in the state. When Kennedy Space Center, known first as Cape Canaveral, was birthed, they had to have a fire department. Where did they get most of their firemen? Why, Sanford, of course. As my mind recalls five or six of our best went to the Cape. That's when I was hired.

The Sanford Fire Department was created in the late 1800's. They were also the ones who created the Sanford Zoo, now called the Central Florida Zoological Park. That all started when someone gave the department a monkey. To this day I do not understand why anybody would give a fire department a monkey. Everybody knows they have a majestic Dalmatian ride on the engines! Oh, well, we never did get a dog. In fact during my tenure someone offered us a Dalmatian, but the chief said, "NO! It will make messes and be a problem."

When I hired on the department there were five men hired at one time to replace those that went to the Cape. I was the second one hired.

The Chief went to the same church that I did and one Sunday he asked me if I would like to work for him. *As I said before, Sanford was a town of approximately 17,000 population and everybody knew everybody else. The Chief knew I did not have a good paying job. I was working night shift for a sand hauling company, working as a mechanic.*

I asked the usual – "How much do you pay."

He asked me how much I was making, then answered my question. His offer was better. You see, I had a wife and two children, had been discharged from the United States Navy for only a short time and needed a better paying job.

When I hired on, I worked every other day and night which was called 72 hours. Later on we worked what we called a KELLY DAY. We worked every other day for six days and then got the seventh day off, which gave us two days off in a row. Later on a bill was passed - *I think it was by the federal government* - which restricted us to only 56 hours a week.

We worked a day and night and then we were off two in a row. Working this kind of shift allowed us to seek part-time employment to supplement our salary, which was not much. Over the years to follow, my salary grew and I did not need to work three jobs to stay alive.

Little boys dream of becoming firemen, but I had never thought about being one in all my twenty-eight years. Someone would call it fate, but I call it faith in God that brought an answer from the Fire Chief for a better paying, more satisfying job.

OK, so much for the formalities. Now let's get on with what this book is all about - **The Fire House Antics!**

I will tell you real life happenings - most happy and funny and some very tragic - so you can see what a firefighter is and why he does what he does.

A FIREFIGHTER is a person who has a lot of compassion for his fellow human beings; he is one who wants to help. And a lot of times he goes out of his way to do so. You'll see that within these pages.

Fire House Antics

First Day on the Job - April Fool's Day

My first day - *I should say the first night* - on the job was one I will never forget. We spent most of the day getting our uniforms and going through the indoctrination process of what to do when the fire bell rings.

Of special importance seemed to be NOT to ride the tailboard of the engine. One of our firemen had been run over when he jumped off of the tailboard thinking the driver had stopped to catch a fire hydrant.

CATCHING A FIRE HYDRANT *is when the engine stops next to the fire hydrant and one of the firefighters gets off, goes to the rear of the engine, removes the gated wye and attaches it to the hydrant. A* GATED WYE *means that each of the hydrant outlets has a ball valve in it so either of the two outlets can be shut off.*

The problem was that the driver was trying to turn around and he backed the engine over him. So we were specifically instructed not to ride the tailboard of the engines.

Most of what we learned was on the job training, because there were no formal schools for firemen. We did have training classes, held at the station, which explained different types of fires (electrical, fuel, wood and paper) and how to fight them without getting hurt.

As I was saying ... my first night at the fire station was memorable, in fact, a comedy. Before we got into bed we took off our boots and our turnout pants, put the boots in the pants so that if we got an alarm at night all we had to do was swing our legs out of bed, stick our feet into the boots, pull up the pants, grab our coat from the floor where we had carefully placed it, pick up our helmet and we were dressed ready to go to the fire.

This night I had done all the proper placement of pants, boots, coat and helmet. Later that night the alarm sounded and yes, I did hear it - *it's hard to sleep with your eyes open.* Anyway, I swung my feet and legs out of bed, put my feet into the boots, and grabbed my coat and helmet.

Now the dormitory did not have heat in it. There was a screen door separating the dorm from the stairway leading to the upper floor of the fire station. When I got to the door I suddenly felt a draft on my legs. I immediately knew I had left my turnout pants and did not get into them. I ran back to my bed looking for my pants.

"If I'm late and don't get on the truck my lieutenant will be sore at me. I can't be late," I thought.

When I reached the side of my bed I could see there were no pants. Now what do I do? At that instant I looked down and there were my pants still around my boots! I hadn't pulled them up!

I pulled them up, buckled them and again ran to the door and slid the pole thinking I would be late. I was the second one on the engine!

P. S. *It was generally a race to see who would be first, and then we could razz the latecomers. And, as soon as the lieutenant and engineer got on the truck, they left the station. If you were not aboard it was your problem.*

True Companions

Early on as a fireman - *I can say "fireman" because there were no women in the profession then* – I learned the meaning of companionship. On my shift (*there were three shifts - A, B and C*) we had two general contractors, two electricians, an electronics nut and me, a former mechanic.

I had worked on semi trucks and trailers as well as working at several new car dealerships. If I wanted anything built, a roof put on my house and (*oh, yes, we also had a plumber*) or most anything else done, I called on my brothers and the work was done. I did the same. If any of my brothers needed car work done I was the one they asked. There were several times I changed an engine or transmission.

I remember my lieutenant had an automatic transmission that was not working properly. He asked me if I knew what might be wrong. I told him that while working at a dealership I had one do the same thing and I fixed it, so I could probably fix his.

My garage is not a mechanic's shop. It is only a car garage, but I had some strong beams that I could use to fashion a lift and pull out an engine, etc. This time, though, I had to jack the car up and make a piece that would hold the transmission from rolling off the jack when we removed it and then reinstalled it.

Working together, we opened the transmission. Sure enough, I found the problem and promptly replaced an inexpensive piece and reinstalled the transmission. It was working when he sold the car.

There were many more times that we helped each other. In fact there is one of my brothers whom I still help and he helps me. He is now a knife maker and gunsmith.

I have to tell one more instance of true companionship. It happened on a New Year's Day. At the time I was stationed at No. 2 Station, an outstation with only three men. This day the lieutenant at HQ station was sick, so the lieutenant from No. 2 had to go to HQ. That left only two of us to man No. 2 Station.

Early that morning just after we went on duty the other fireman suggested we change the springs on his old car. No.2 station never had much to do so we had a lot of time with nothing to do. I agreed. "Why not! We can get it done in a couple hours."

We were allowed to work on our cars after hours and on weekends and holidays. So we got a bumper jack from the old car, jacked the rear end of it up and placed cement blocks under the frame to hold it safely. After all, we were firefighters, advocates of safety.

Well, we got it safely in the air and began taking the springs out from under it. We had no problems. All the nuts and bolts came out without a problem. We then installed the new springs.

At noon my wife brought over some black-eyed peas and hog jowls. You know, for good luck the coming year. Also, along with that she had some sauerkraut and pork - *the northern version of a good luck meal* - so we had a double dose of good luck coming.

We had started to take the car off the blocks and the other fireman was under the car removing the blocks when my wife came

Fire House Antics

with all this food for our lunch. About this time the jack gave way and the car fell on the other firefighter.

Now get this picture: two of us manning a fire station with one of them trapped under his own car. I expected a fire call any minute.

I hollered to my wife to call the ambulance. I thought the car had killed him.

He kept hollering at me to get a jack and jack the car up so he could get out. *I forgot to tell you why the car fell on him. You see, I used the bumper jack we had used before, but this time it did not hold and the car came down on him.*

I was running around without directions trying to find a jack when **the fire bell sounded**. Now do you think I'm rational at this point? It took moments but I finally had enough sense to run to my car and get the jack from the truck, jack the car up and release my trapped brother.

About this time all the trucks from HQ came charging into the station and wondering what's going on – *my wife's phone call!*. My 'brother' is walking around now, stretching and giving me what for for letting the car fall on him.

Actually he was joking, but I didn't know how hurt he was. He said he was OK so the trucks returned to HQ station and we went inside, ate lunch and watched TV the rest of the day.

That evening he took a shower and got ready for bed and so did I. When I came from the shower he was lying on the couch sleeping so I went on to bed. Later that night I awoke and went to his bed to check on him; he wasn't there. I then went to the TV room and there he was lying on the couch with his hands on his chest. He looked as dead as any corpse I had ever seen, so I put my ear to his nose to listen for breathing. Praise the Lord! He was alive, so I went back to bed.

The next morning he asked me if I thought he had died and then he began laughing.

He had been awake and I didn't know it when I checked on him that night.

Dispatch Duty

Each day we were on duty we were assigned to one of the engines or we had station duty. STATION DUTY consisted of answering the fire phone as well as the SUGAR LINE as we called it and also manning the radio for communications. If the fire phone rang, it also rang a bell in the dorm. We had to answer the phone by the second ring or we heard it from the chief. Whenever it rang there was a mad rush to get to your assigned place.

The station man or DISPATCHER had to sit there at the radio and phones all day. He had to get a relief so he could eat or go to the bathroom.

At that time there was only one sugar line and if the chief tried to call and it was busy, he would call on the fire phone knowing everybody would go to their respective duty station and leave the sugar line empty. He wouldn't say a word but would hang up and call on the sugar line again. He thought he was crafty, but the next story, I think, shows that we were craftier than he.

Each day he would come to the station at 8:00 a.m. and back his car into the station or leave it on the driveway apron out front. Then he'd walk to the center post (between the two bays) of the building where there was a thermometer. He would check the temperature and then check his watch against the station clock, which was Western Union time - *the correct time, I think.*

Everyday he did this. It was a ritual.

Charles L. Bose

  One day we took a cigarette lighter and really heated up the thermometer. When he came in and checked the temperature he said, "It's hot, but still seems rather cool."

  We would from time to time pull this prank on the chief. I'm not sure if we were getting away with fooling him or if he was just going along with the prank. In any case we thought we were pulling something on him, and we were having fun and a good laugh doing it. Chief probably said to himself, "If they only knew that I know".

The First Water Rescue

The first water rescue made by the Sanford Fire Department was on Lake Monroe. We got a call one evening that a car had driven into the lake. We all knew that we didn't have any equipment for water rescue. It had not even been discussed as a need. So here we were, going to a water rescue with only a hank of rope, an extension ladder and guts.

When we arrived, we saw the car about 100 feet out from the sea wall. *The sea wall had been built in the 1920's by the CCC or WPA, all along the south shore of Lake Monroe in the city limits.* We called the Seminole County Fire Department, which had a couple of trained divers, but we had no way to get to the car.

I saw one of the city commissioners and asked him to go to my house and get the canoe from the back yard. In a few minutes he came with the canoe and we launched it by dropping it over the sea wall and going down the ladder to get into it. The driver was still in the vehicle as we did all this. Finally the divers came and went into the water and swam to the car.

The car was in water about eight feet deep. The lake is a shallow lake, so it was not hard to reach. What made it bad was that the water was murky because the car had hit bottom.

As we got into the canoe - *can you imagine a rescue from a canoe!* - a helicopter from the neighboring county came to the scene. It was welcomed mainly for the light that it had. It lit up the whole area.

While one of the firefighters and I were in the canoe trying to drag a cable from a tow truck to the car, the divers found the lady trapped in the auto. They didn't expect her to be alive as too much time had passed, but they took her to the hospital anyway where she was pronounced DOA.

Back at the scene the two of us in a canoe were paddling as hard as we could to get the cable to the divers. They would attach it to the car so it could be dragged ashore. All this time the helicopter, hovering maybe fifty feet above us, created a terrible amount of turbulence and an almost impossible situation. I kept waving my paddle at them and hollering. Finally they decided they were doing more harm than good and stationed themselves further away so the light was more efficient and there was little down-wash from the chopper blades.

We did get the auto out of the water and the city commissioner took my canoe back to my home. That was our first attempt at a water rescue, and though a life was lost, the experience paved the way for better equipment and training to come.

The Old Ladder Truck

There was the time we had a call to one of the local middle schools. It was protocol for the ladder truck to respond to all schools, hospitals, nursing homes and the downtown area. This day I was assigned to the ladder truck.

In order to get the truck out of the station, without hitting a car parked across the street, you had to start turning the steering wheel as soon as you felt the rear wheels hit the street at the end of the station driveway. If you didn't do it exactly you would hit any car parked across the street. Well, as you might guess, I didn't turn in time and I put a dent in the bumper of a car.

The owner was standing on the sidewalk watching me. I told her, "Stay there with the car; I'll be back soon."

We proceeded to the school and on arrival were told there was no fire and to return to station. I told the lieutenant I needed to talk to the chief. He asked why and I told him that I had hit a car. He said to go back to the station and call the police.

I went back to the station and there, standing by her car, was the lady. I called the police and they came by and made an accident report. I had to write a lengthy report how the accident happened and how it would be avoided next time. I made a report with drawings and measurements and found out you couldn't get the truck out of the station without hitting a car parked across the street.

The city bought her a new bumper. They did not restrict parking in front of the station though. We just had to be very careful when we exited the station with the ladder truck.

All this changed when we moved to a new station house a few years later.

Haunted

As I said, we were assigned dispatcher (station duty) on a rotating basis. This next story is about one of the firefighters who was rather squeamish about being alone in the firehouse.

*It was said the firehouse was haunted. There had been a hanging many years before in the alley behind the station. Maybe the old station **was** haunted.*

Anyway, this particular day he had station duty. That night we had a fire. *After we extinguished a fire we always called the station and gave a 10-98-19, meaning we were finished and returning to station.* We called several times but no one responded. We didn't know what was happening, so we drove a little faster, returning only to find him standing in the middle of the street as white as a ghost.

We asked him what was wrong and he said he was not going to be in the station alone again. He said he heard someone walking up the stairs to the dorm but nobody was there. He'd looked.

To add credence to his story: During winter all the heat we had downstairs was a fireplace in one corner of the station. Wood was used in large quantities to keep the trucks and us warm.

We spent large quantities of time sitting around the fireplace talking and studying our streets and hydrants. Often we left the chairs in a neat semicircle and went to bed. The next morning the chairs would be in disarray and nobody had messed with them!

The old station building was later sold and the people who own it now still hear sounds and strange things still happen.

Charles L. Bose

More Pranks

We had a fireplace downstairs but we also had a pot-bellied stove used to heat the dorm at night. (*It doesn't stay cold in Florida for long but we do have some cold, cold nights.*) Most nights someone would get up and open one of the windows and nearly freeze everybody else. The excuse was always either "I'm hot." or "It's too stuffy!" *Actually, the culprit was doing it for a laugh and to have some fun, anything to cause a stir among the men.*

I guess the question arises, "Why do you act so silly and do such foolish things?"

When you go to a fire or rescue and there are people who are hurt or who perish, it is hard for a person to forget. If it were once, it would be quite different, but when that is your job and it happens every day, you have to do something to rid your mind of the memories.

If we hadn't been able to escape the memories, I would never have worked so long as a fireman.

Charles L. Bose

Big Guns

Our 'B' shift was probably the worst shift for doing ornery things. I remember "Big Bertha" as one of our special times.

"Big Bertha" was a piece of galvanized pipe four inches in diameter and approximately four feet long. We made a carbide cannon with it.

We took a 2x4 six inches long and drove it into one end of the pipe for a wood plug. *I do NOT recommend anybody doing this as it can be very dangerous, but we lived on the edge anyway so we did not have any trouble dealing with the possibility of it exploding.*

After inserting the 2x4 we drilled a hole about 8" from the plug. This was a touch hole. Then we put some granules of carbide in along with a small amount of water; the two mixed and created acetylene gas - *very explosive*. We would put a tin can in the other end to act as a projectile. This whole concoction was clamped in the mechanics vice with the end facing the alley running behind the station.

We did this only at night under the blanket of darkness when there were fewer police on duty. When we lit a match and placed it at the touchhole, the alley lit up like day and the most awful roar you ever heard shattered the night.

We only did this once a night for fear of getting caught. We kept Bertha hidden under the work bench out of sight and when she roared, everybody would run as fast as they could up to the dorm and

Charles L. Bose

jump in bed, clothes and all, in case the police came to investigate the explosion.

We never did get caught.

P. S. One day the manager from the furniture store came over and told how, on many mornings when he opened up, he would find pictures that had been hanging on the wall, now on the floor. We assured him we knew nothing about it or why the pictures were on the floor. Must be ghosts!

The police department didn't trust us at all. In fact, the police chief told his officers not to hang around the fire department. He said we would get them into trouble. Now you know we would not have done that, at least not on purpose!

Electricians Union Hall

There was one time - *one of many* - that the police came to the department wondering what was happening. This particular time was when we "unloaded" the Electrical Workers Union Hall. The Union Hall was just across the street from the department and the workers had meetings once a month.

We knew a lot of the members as Sanford was a small town and everybody knew everybody. This night we got word that the electrical workers were going to vote to go on strike. As the union members began to assemble, we watched their upper floor from the upper floor of the station.

It seems that there were always fireworks of some sort hidden in someone's locker at the fire department. Cherry bombs and M-80's were our favorites. Who knew when you might need a cherry bomb?

When the hall was full we opened an upstairs window. One of the firemen took out a slingshot, inserted a cherry bomb and drew it well behind his ear. Then he told us to light it and say, "OK" when it was lit. He then let go and the cherry bomb sailed across the road and behind the union hall and exploded.

I guess the union members thought they had been bombed. They came out of that hall so fast. It's a wonder someone was not hurt. They stood around for a few minutes before reentering the hall, taking time to reassure each other that they had not been bombed.

Charles L. Bose

P. S. We used to set bottle rockets into the restroom when someone was in there. We also planted M-80's in the flowerpots along First Street using a cigarette pushed over the fuse (time delay).

P.P.S. The U.S.O. was located just about a block away from the station. Many a night we went to the roof of the station and, using the same sling shot, shot fire crackers over there.

Shower Problems

Taking a shower or going to the bathroom always presented a problem. There were so few of us that if one person did not make it to a fire or rescue it left a large hole. I remember several times I saw the fellows come down the pole partly dressed, one even brought his sheet off the bed with him. He looked like Superman!

We all hated to take a shower because, sure enough, just as you got all lathered up, the fire phone would ring and you had to get into your bunker gear wet and soapy, to say nothing about having to drive a truck or fight a fire dripping wet.

There was a time like that for me when I was driving the ladder truck. I put off taking a shower as long as I could. Finally I got in and got real soapy when the bell rang and I had to go. I came out of the shower and stepped into my boots and jerked up my pants. As I jerked them up the whole crotch of the pants ripped out, leaving me there with me hanging out.

I didn't stop. I kept on going, slid the pole, ran to the ladder truck and pulled out of the station. My soapy hands slipped and slid on the wheel, but I managed to handle the truck to the fire.

When we arrived, I was asked to get out and do something. I answered, "I'd like to, but I can't."

"Why?" they asked.

"Well, you see, the bottom of my turnout pants doesn't exist!"

"Oh," was the reply. "Why don't you go back and take care of the problem."

Charles L. Bose

    I said I would be glad to and did.

    When the fire was out and the shift returned to quarters, I was given a better pair until new ones could be ordered.

Beach Buggy

I spoke before about our being able to work on our own cars after hours, weekends and holidays. Well, we built three or four of what we called "beach buggies".

We would buy an old model Ford, chop the body off, take the seats off, and then cut about 2-3 feet out of the middle of the frame and re-weld it in place. Then we'd shorten the drive shaft and re-weld it. We'd then make some sort of body out of wood. We would drive these "beach buggies" up and down the beach at Daytona or New Smyrna, or we would use them to drive through the woods for the fun of it.

These "cars" had to be road worthy, meaning they had to have all the safety things: lights, wipers, brakes, emergency brake, etc., if they were to be driven on the highways. My lieutenant and I built one for him. It was a slick machine and quite fast. He drove it everywhere till one night he was coming back around the lakefront and he met another car head on. My lieutenant was killed instantly.

The police found me at home and I had to go verify the fact that the car had lights and that they worked. The beach buggy was demolished in the wreck, and since it was homemade, there was a question as to whether the vehicle had lights and if they worked. The lights did work because I put them on and wired them.

The Lieutenant and I were very close. I still miss him and the good times we shared.

Charles L. Bose

Fire House Antics

Bulk Plant Fire

I want to tell you about a bulk fuel plant fire and the detective work that is sometimes involved in a fire.

It was a normal day *and night* at the fire department; we were eating too much, watching TV and generally picking on each other.

I always stayed up late to call my wife before I went to bed. She had to take care of our children, but at 11:00 each night she was free to talk. This night was no different than the others. I sat up and watched the TV news and weather. They said there was a thunderstorm coming from Daytona traveling at approximately 5 miles per hour (Daytona is 45 miles NE of Sanford.).

I thought, "So what! Just another storm! They're not unusual in Florida."

I got up, turned off the TV and was walking down the hall to my bed, when I heard this sound like thunder. I thought, "If that storm is traveling at 5 mph from Daytona and it's 45 miles to Daytona, something is wrong!"

About that time the fire phone rang. It was the police reporting that the Phillips Petroleum plant was on fire.

By this time my shift personnel were at my side asking, "What's wrong?" "Where do we go?" "What trucks do you want?" "Where do I go?" "What do I do?" etc.

The shift lieutenant was off duty that day, leaving me the next senior man in charge of the shift. I told the men to get on the trucks assigned to them and go to the bulk plant and more decisions would be made there.

As we pulled out of the station and looked north (the direction of the fire) all downtown was lit up. It looked like daytime. Needless to say, when I saw this, the adrenalin started to flow. When we reached the site of the fire, which was fourteen blocks from the station, my driver asked me what to do. I said, "Put water on it, all you can get. Hook up to as many fire hydrants as possible."

There was a tanker truck hooked by hose to the off loading ramp. We unhooked it and drove it away - *luckily the keys were still in the ignition.* I'm not sure where the driver was.

All this time large columns of fire were coming from the fuel tanks and the tanks were whistling as they vented. It was an awful sound, a very shrill whistle.

We are taught: Never put the flame of a burning tank out. Cool the tank with water and as it cools, the flame will go out and not create a new hazard. So, we put mega amounts of water on these tanks.

It takes a lot of water and a lot of time to cool a 50,000-gallon fuel tank and we had four of them to deal with. Once we got water flowing, all of us felt some relief and started to relax a bit. We were there well past the time the sun comes up.

You must wonder why we used water and not foam. Well, there is another avenue of attack to a fire of this kind. It is to use foam, but the fuel must be in the shape of a pond and not inside a tank. The foam covers the fuel suffocating it.

Fire House Antics

Now for the reason for the fire: As daylight came, my lieutenant, the chief and the fire marshal came to the scene to investigate. My lieutenant and I started looking for a reason.

There was a house one block away. We went to see if they had any damage. They allowed us in the house and as we looked about I notice some ball fringe on a curtain hanging outside a glass pane of the front window.

I commented to the lieutenant that there must have been an explosion inside the house to bend the glass and allow the fringe to be blown outside. The owner of the house said, "You should see the wall back at the hot water heater. It moved the wall three inches." We went to look at it and found the water heater was gas operated.

Now the night before it had been rainy and the air was heavy. There were fumes coming from the semi off-loading at the fuel plant. The fumes traveled all over the ground - you could see the burnt patches of grass. They led to the house and into the house where the gas water heater had ignited the fumes, which led back to the tanks.

There was no explosion at the tanks. The tanks had safety vents on top which were being opened by the expanding gases, causing this thunder-like noise. The most we had to deal with was fire at the relief valve on top of each storage tank.

Charles L. Bose

Fire House Antics

Bats in the Dorm

The time a bat got into the dorm caused a lot of excitement. We had a large fan in the rear of the dorm in one of the windows. This day, when we were sitting in the dorm watching television, a bat came through the fan and started chasing one of the men around the lockers.

We had a row of lockers down the middle of the dorm and our beds were on the sidewalls of the dorm. You could walk around and around, except this time he ran around and around.

Everybody took shelter: some in office rooms, some in the restroom, except me. I stood there and watched as the fireman ran around the lockers while hollering for someone to kill the bat. Around he would go, again and again, hollering the same. This went on for several minutes. Around and around. It was kind of funny.

I'm not sure how he wanted me to kill the bat. I didn't have a gun and couldn't have used it if I had. So ... the last time he came around - *there were many* - I opened a door and the bat flew in with me right after him.

I slammed the door, shutting it behind me, and my eyes fell upon this 2x4 about six feet long. I'm not sure why it was there, but there it was. I grabbed it, swung and knocked that bat out of the air on the first try. Beginner's luck! I killed it, and then we had a funeral for it.

To remember that fireman running around those lockers with his eyes bugging out and him yelling – well, it makes me laugh today.

Charles L. Bose

It wasn't very funny for him though. We later learned he was **very** afraid of bats.

Being Timed

There was a barbershop across the street from the station and the owner had at one time been a volunteer fireman for the city. He used to come over to the station in the evening along with another older gentleman who once was the assistant chief of the department. They would come by at least once a week and play pool.

We had a pool table in the dorm and every night there was a game going on. Once in a while we would have a tournament. Some of the games got rather heated but at the end all was well. There was many a meal and game that was interrupted by the fire bell and many a meal eaten cold when we returned to quarters. But that was our job and we loved it.

This same barber would time us from the time he heard the bell to the time we exited the station. Usually it took less than three minutes during the day. He couldn't time us at night - *he wasn't in his shop* - but I'll bet it didn't take any longer at night than during the day.

Charles L. Bose

Brush Truck

We had an old Dodge power wagon - military surplus - that we used as a brush truck. It was a four-wheel drive and very powerful. I think it would have climbed a tree.

One day we were going to a brush fire and I was driving. I was headed south on Sanford Avenue when I looked out the side window and saw this tire and wheel just rolling right along past me.

It didn't take long to find out where it came from! The axle had broken and wheel, tire and axle had come out of the rear end of that old truck.

We called the station by radio and told them to dispatch another truck. There we sat by the roadside – after chasing down the tire and wheel, of course – waiting to be rescued.

Charles L. Bose

Fire House Cooking

Let me tell you about my favorite time at the station - **lunch**!

On each shift there was one self-appointed cook. What a cook ours was! I know, I ate on all three shifts. I was partial to ours though. He did all the cooking and when he was done, we (the rest of the shift) would clean up and wash all the dishes. What a mess! He generally used all the pots and pans that were in the cabinets!

We did **not** eat sandwiches. We ate **MEALS** and we had such things as Mexican cornbread, made with hamburger, Velveeta cheese, bell peppers, corn bread mix, onions, etc. We made it in a 9x12 pan.

Usually we made two of them so we would have enough for supper. One pan would usually feed all seven of us. We also had a salad and some kind of pie or cake. We could make cakes but not pies; we bought them.

Now, there was a time when you did not have to pay to talk to the telephone operator. You could call information and ask an operator for a telephone number if you couldn't find it in the book. We often called the operator in Alaska and talked to her about the weather.

To get back to the kitchen, we could make a cake 'cause anybody can open a box! This day we decided to make a cake and, oh, boy! did it look good! But we didn't know how to make frosting. This was before IF (instant frosting).

We thought and thought about how to make frosting. Finally I said, "I know how to find out."

"How?" they asked.

"I'll call the information operator!"

I called and asked her if she was the information operator and she assured me she was. So I asked her if she could tell me how to make frosting for a cake. *I had told her who I was and where I was calling from.*

She said, "Just a minute." and left the phone. Meantime I told someone to get a paper and pencil to copy as I talked.

Shortly she came back on the phone and read me a recipe for frosting. I thanked her and we made the frosting as she instructed. It came out just perfect. We iced the cake and then feasted on it.

When we made chili, which was generally in the winter, we would make a pot that was of the largest kind. We ate out of serving bowls and used quart jars for our tea. We always made iced tea for every meal, even in the winter. It's a Southern thing!

We also had a dish called "rolled steak". I start salivating just thinking about it. You get steak cut very thin and then cut it into strips 2-3 inches wide, maybe 4-5 inches long. Place a quarter of an onion on each strip and roll the steak around the onion. Then take a strip of bacon and wrap it around the steak and hold it with a toothpick.

After making many of these you fry them in a skillet - *cast iron does best* - till nearly done. Then place them in a pot and use the drippings to make a full skillet of gravy. Place the gravy in the pot along with the steak rolls and again heat. Cook until done, adding water as needed to keep the gravy from getting too thick. This is fit for a king to eat.

During my tenure we had several people ask if they could eat with us, including the city mayor, several local pastors and city commissioners. The chief ate with us at least once a week.

On occasion we would go to the beach and catch silver mullet with a cast net, go shrimping or get oysters, and we always had a good meal that day. Some of us would go to the coast in the evening and go shrimping. What a meal that would make for us! We could catch thirty to forty pounds in an evening using a net.

One day we had a bushel of oysters. We wanted to steam them but some of the fellows wanted oyster soup. So we had soup, steamed oysters, fried oysters and some raw.

To steam the oysters we went out behind the station on a grassy area, took some bricks or cement block, whichever was available, and made a fire pit. We then took a piece of expanded metal, placed it on top of the bricks and build a fire under it.

We would spread the oysters on the expanded metal and place a wet croaker bag on them to create steam. The steam would then cook the oysters just perfectly. *A CROAKER BAG is the same as a burlap feed sack. We in the South call them croaker bags because that is what you used to carry the frogs you caught frog gigging.*

I can say we always ate well and it never did cost much per day... maybe five dollars for two large meals.

Charles L. Bose

Banana Pudding

Once, my best friend and I decided to make some banana pudding. We went to the grocery store and bought bananas, vanilla pudding and vanilla wafers. With all the ingredients in hand we set about to make a pan of pudding.

Now, mind you, this was not a small pan. Rather it was one of those 9" x 12" x 2" deep pans. Everybody wanted to get into the act, but we said we bought the stuff and **we** were going to eat it.

When the pudding was done cooking, we sat down to the table and began eating, laughing and talking till it was all gone. The rest of the fellows asked if we had eaten it all. We assured them we had and had even washed the pan. Oh, it was so good!

Later that evening both of us became very sick. Everybody just laughed at us, while we were about to die! To this day I do not have much of an appetite for banana pudding.

Both of us learned two good lessons that day: NOT TO BE A GLUTTON and ALWAYS SHARE WITH OTHERS.

Charles L. Bose

Old #1

We used to have two old American LaFrance fire engines. They were a 1920 and a 1921, but age does not make any difference to the story. They were old with right hand steering, one to one steering ratio - *meaning whatever amount you turned the steering wheel, the wheels turned the same amount* - chain drive and no cab.

The engine was huge. The battery was dead most of the time, which meant we had to hand-crank it. In order to crank it, you had to push the compression release and pull the crank. What a noise it would make in the station!

We had to move it every Thursday. That was clean-up day. We had to scrub the apparatus floor. So every week we would crank-up old #2 and drive it outside so we could sweep and mop under her.

This one day my lieutenant said, "Why not go for a ride along the lakefront (in old #2)." I was second in command and thought it a novel idea. All the trucks needed to be kept running. If they were in the station, they were in service. This was a working fire engine, just very old and antiquated.

We drove old #2 down to the lake and Lieutenant was driving. During the short trip to the lake he suggested to me that we find out how fast she could go. *Understand this is not a racecar or truck and it is not intended to go fast but to pump water in order to extinguish fires.* Still I kind of liked the idea of finding out how fast she could go without falling apart.

Charles L. Bose

It didn't take long for us to find out with the air and bugs blowing in our face. We managed to get a glimpse of the speedometer as it reached 70 mph.

I think now how foolish we were, but it still was fun. It certainly was not very stable on the road at that speed.

P.S. The truck is, as of this writing, at #3 Station being rebuilt. We used to drive it in the Christmas parade and the kids loved it.

Fire House Antics

Superball and Frisbee

There just wasn't much for us to do on weekends but sit out front and watch the world go by. The station was three doors off First Street, so people would come by and talk.

One of our pastimes was throwing a superball. The building across the street had a large brick wall with no windows, which gave us something to throw at. It was like a jai alai fronton. You would throw it as hard as you could and it came back many times faster.

The object was to catch the ball on return so it didn't break windows on our side. We were lucky no windows were ever broken, but we did loose a couple balls. One I remember in particular.

We had been throwing it for quite some time and we were not paying much attention to traffic, when all of a sudden, a car came by and the ball got stuck under the car. The last we saw that ball it was bouncing under the car as it was driven down the street. I often wonder how long it stayed under the car and what it sounded like from inside the car.

Another game we played was throwing the Frisbee. The Chief did not care too much for our doing this, so we would wait till the weekend when he was not around. He also was insistent that we wear our caps and shirts if we were outside the station, but in the summer here in Florida it gets rather hot. We didn't have air-conditioning until many years after I started.

Charles L. Bose

We would suffer the day until the chief went home. Then off came the caps and shirts. We sure did enjoy throwing the Frisbee from one end of the block to the other.

Actually we closed the street in front of the station when we played in it. Nobody seemed to care. Everybody knew that we had nothing to do but wait for an emergency. We were doing no harm to anybody, just amusing ourselves. In fact several times people would stop and sit on the benches, watching and encouraging us.

This was all good, but one Sunday we were throwing the Frisbee when all of a sudden we heard someone yelling. We looked and saw Chief riding in a car down First Street. Actually he was hanging out of the window; he was as mad as a hornet telling us to get inside the station and get into uniform!

As soon as he got to the house he called on the phone and really chewed us out, saying he better never catch us doing that again. He was afraid we would give him, the department and the city a bad name.

Packing House Fire

When I started working as a firefighter we only fought fires. We didn't do any EMS work at all. It was only because of a TV program filmed in California that we started doing EMS work. Back then all EMS work was taken care of by the ambulance companies which were run by the funeral homes and some private ambulance firms.

We used to have approximately 30-40 fires a month. Now, I'm told that they have nearly that many runs a day, mostly EMS.

There was a fruit-packing house located just off routes 17 and 92 and across from the station. It was called the Skinner Building, named after a man named Skinner.

One night it caught fire and we rolled out of the station to a ball of flames across the street. The fire accelerated very rapidly because of all the paraffin that was on the floor. *Paraffin was used to do something with the fruit.* The floor was soaked with it.

We had engines coming from HQ including old #2, which sounded, as I heard it coming, like a tank. We had two and a half inch supply lines hooked to every fire hydrant within a two block area.

Believe me, there was fire everywhere and everyone was working as hard as they could. The whole building was wooden so you can see that there was an abundant amount of fuel for the fire.

I mentioned a 2 ½" line; it will flow 250 gallons per minute at 120 psi pressure. That does not seem like a big deal, but, in fact, it is nearly impossible to hold unless you put an S in the hose, then you can hold it. Problem is - you cannot move it then. The weight of the hose and the water make it impossible. You just have to stand there and wave it around as much as you can without losing it. If you loose it, it becomes a wild snake, swishing around. The possibilities of getting hurt are almost certain, so you hang on to it and hope someone comes by and relieves you.

I remember manning a 2 ½" line for nearly an hour and not being able to move. A 1" line is much lighter and full of much less water. You can walk around with it. But I sat on the line till someone came and relieved me. Believe me, I was ready for relief.

We pumped and pumped water and fought as hard as we could. One of the men who had worked his way into the building was just spraying water all about when he finally said, "I think I've got it blacked out now". (*He didn't see any fire.*) Then he looked up and saw the sky. He thought he had saved the building when, in fact, it had burned down around him.

Procedure required that if we were off-duty and were going out of town we were required to call in and get permission to leave town. This was one of the few times that we had a call-up. All those off-duty were called into duty.

Asleep at the Wheel

I remember one time we got a call in the night and we all hit the pole; down we slid and ran to the engine. The lieutenant and engineer both got aboard and pulled out of the station. It was an open cab truck so the jump-seat riders generally would turn around and talk to the lieutenant and engineer.

The engineer was the driver. He was responsible for driving to the fire without incident, locate the fire hydrant, set up the engine to pump configuration and be able to maintain proper pressure on the hand lines. These were 1" lines with 95 gpm fog nozzles.

I noticed as we were driving down Sanford Avenue that we were going only 15-20 mph, when usually 30 to 40 would be the normal speed. The lieutenant was just sitting there looking straight ahead.

All of a sudden the engineer's head jerked around and he said to the lieutenant, "Where the —— are we going?" The lieutenant told him the address and the driver immediately shifted gears. We were off to the races, uh, I mean fire.

Later I asked the engineer what was wrong with him. "I was asleep," he answered.

Now, it's not easy to be awakened in the middle of the night and be fully functional. Knowing all the hydrants and streets, let alone being able to drive, set up the pump, etc. or, as an EMT or paramedic, to be able to do the correct thing or do the correct procedure the correct way is a challenge when you're **not** tired.

Charles L. Bose

In Sanford we were able to go from the station to the furthest end of town in approximately ten minutes. That's **not** a lot of time to become completely awake.

Cooking

Though I've told before about cooking in the firehouse, this incident will thrill anybody who has ever used a pressure cooker. I know now the reason some people are afraid to use them. The best thing about using one *(and most know this)* is it's a way to cook fast and make tough meat tender.

Well, this day the cook decided to prepare chicken potpie. He also wanted to cook the chicken fast. I guess he was starting late; he had some reason, good or bad. Anyway, he put the chicken in the pressure cooker to cook and left the kitchen.

We all know it's not wise to leave pots cooking on the stove. Usually, whatever is in them burns, but that was not the situation here.

During the cook's absence one of the members of the staff, a training officer, came to the kitchen to see what was for lunch. *Generally the staff ate with us.* He went to the pressure cooker. This one did not have a gauge on top, but just one of those circular weights that jump about as the steam escapes.

The officer, for reasons unknown to him or anybody alive, lifted the weight off the little spout that it sat upon.

Now I'm not sure if I have to elaborate on what happened next. I'm sure some of you know, but for the sake of those who do not, I will tell the rest of the story. First of all, we did not have pot pie that day!

Charles L. Bose

When he lifted the weight off, the steam, water, chicken meat, chicken bones and all in the cooker came out of that little hole. Where did it go? All over the kitchen - mostly on the ceiling.

The clean up lasted for several hours using all hands including the training officer's. He often spoke of that incident later and could not come up with a reasonable explanation for lifting the weight off the spout.

We probably had sandwiches for lunch that day, I don't remember. For sure, we ate something and by the time the mess was cleaned, **anything** would have tasted good.

Fire House Antics

Charles L. Bose

Car Wreck

The following story I would rather forget, but for the sake of this writing, I will retell it and then I can put it to rest. It isn't good for us to dwell on sad incidents.

To begin, we got a call one evening, (*I'm not sure of the time*) reporting an awful wreck at Five Points and one of our police officers was involved. Five Points was approximately three miles out of town. At this time we were not allowed to go to anything outside the city limits unless personnel or property of the city were involved. The police department had called in the alarm.

That day the police had been involved in a cat and mouse chase with a car and driver. The police were having a time keeping up with him so they could stop and arrest him, that is, until he got on 17-92, a state highway going through town.

They chased him out of town trying to catch him. It was later determined that he was going at least 117 mph when he collided with a large Oldsmobile entering the highway. The auto held a police officer and his wife, on their way home from a party. The car being chased (a Trans-Am) hit the other with such force that it cut the Olds in half, killing both driver and passenger.

When we got the call I was at #2 Station with one other fireman. We didn't like going to accidents for fear of death. We could handle injury okay. Usually we could bandage, etc. to help the victims.

Charles L. Bose

Driving to the accident we didn't say a word to each other. As we came to the accident there were blue lights enough to make K-Mart jealous.

As I said, this Trans-Am was traveling at such speed that it literally cut the Olds in half, killing both the driver and his wife. The driver of the Trans AM was also dead, but his wife and their child, whom she was holding on her lap, survived.

We were asked to help pick up body pieces of the dead officer and his wife and put them in body bags. After we gathered up all the parts and pieces, we took our booster hose and washed the rest down the drain. We went to look at the Trans-Am during the pickup process and found the police officer's head sitting on the hood. The force was so great ...

I'm sorry for the graphic detail, but without it, it would seem just another accident.

Perhaps by telling about this tragic event you can understand how we feel about what we do. I was not able to eat for several days for the smell of death and blood stayed with me. This wreck was the worst thing that my eyes have ever seen. I pray I never have to see a similar incident again.

Does this story help you understand better what I said in MORE PRANKS. I hope so. We do crazy things to retain our sanity and escape from the memories.

City Worker Scalded

We had a call one day to the edge of town to a sewer lift station near a subdivision of homes. Seems that a city worker was there doing some work on the faulty lift station when he was scalded by steam. I'm not sure what or why it happened but it did. When we arrived on the scene the fellow was running around like a chicken with its head cut off, hollering and screaming.

There is a protocol to follow in medicine and in this case we were supposed to administer oxygen to the patient. I would have if I could have caught him and held on to him! He was much larger than I was and I was not in the mood to get hurt that day.

We finally talked him into getting into the engine and we would take him to the hospital in lieu of waiting for the ambulance. My driver started to get under the wheel when I told him to hold the worker and I would drive. He did as directed and away we went.

I passed the station at about sixty miles an hour - about as fast as that engine would go, sirens blaring. We arrived at the hospital and were met by nurses and a doctor who took the fellow inside and started treating him.

We went back to the station where we were chewed out by one of the EMT's for not following protocol. We had a few words till the chief came and told us we did the correct thing. Later we got word from the hospital that what we did had saved the man's life.

Charles L. Bose

CPR – My First Time

Saving life reminds me of the first time I used CPR (cardio-pulmonary resuscitation). It happened one day as we were fooling around, which was most of the time. We received an alarm about a man down in the Winn Dixie grocery parking lot. This was just one block away so it didn't take long to get there.

When we arrived the man was lying on the sidewalk in front of the store. I checked for breathing and he wasn't. The next move was to start CPR. As we administered CPR the fellow's eyes opened and he looked at me as if to say "thank you so much."

I continued CPR until the ambulance came minutes after our arrival. We put him on a gurney and as we did, he died again. Again I started CPR and again he awoke with the same look; but the fourth time we lost him, he did not respond. I feel even now as though he told me "thanks".

What a reward for the efforts made for him. Later, the doctor in the emergency room said the man had hardening of the arteries and at his age there was no way we could have saved him.

On the other side of the coin there were many on whom we used CPR who survived.

One of the most frustrating incidents on the job happened in the middle of the night when we got a call to a "person down". I'm not sure yet what they mean by "person down" when most of the time they were in chairs, cars, etc. Anyway, this particular night, about 3:00 a.m., we got a call of a "person down".

Charles L. Bose

We jumped out of bed into our turnout gear, ran to the truck and across town we sped, not knowing what awaited us.

Upon our arrival at the address I had to get the trauma and O_2 bags, jump a ditch and enter the house. By this time I was huffing and puffing.

The house was full of people as though they were having a party.

"Who is the sick person?" I asked, panting.

A lady said she was. I started asking questions like "What's wrong with you?"

"My tummy hurts."

"How long has it hurt?"

"Three days."

I told her it was three in the morning and she had gotten us out of bed. "Why did you call us at this hour?"

"My tummy hurts bad."

"Did you have a bowel movement?"

"Yes."

"When?"

"Today."

I wasn't getting any place.

She looked fine; her vitals were normal, so I asked if anybody in the room could drive. Everybody held up a hand so I asked, "Would somebody take this person to the ER at the hospital?" Someone said he would do it in lieu of an ambulance bill.

Fire House Antics

P. S. Often we were awakened out of a sleep to go to someone who wanted immediate attention rather than wait till the next day to see a physician. We were not allowed as EMT's to administer even an aspirin; the most we could administer was O_2. It was always frustrating.

Charles L. Bose

Fire House Antics

One of Our Own Killed, One Injured

There was a fire downtown one evening about 6:00 pm. I remember because I was at church for our Wednesday night supper and prayer meeting.

This evening I was just hanging around talking when I heard the fire sirens and then saw the trucks go past the church. I didn't pay much attention as sirens were a part of my life and I had long since given up following the trucks. That would only bring a lot of work and no pay, so I just didn't pay any more attention to the sirens.

All of a sudden one of the city commissioners, who belonged to the church, came running into the fellowship hall where I was and told me that the building next to a paint store downtown was on fire. Now, just because he told me didn't mean that I had to go to the fire, but the way he was looking at me, I knew I'd better go. His eyes were large and pleading, so I decided to see what was going on.

I didn't have any of my turnout gear and I knew there wouldn't be any spare on the trucks but I ran three blocks to where I found one of my fellow firefights alone and wide eyed. He had driven one of the older pumpers and there was nobody to help him hook up. When I came into sight, he hollered at me to help him.

"Are you alone?" I yelled.

"Yes!" he hollered back. *I might add it was not just yes; there was more to it.* Anyway, he asked me to help him hook to a hydrant and pull some hand line to the fire. I had to pull approximately one hundred feet of 2 ½" hose to the hydrant.

Charles L. Bose

I turned the hydrant on because I knew from our training that he had hooked the hose to the inlet side of the pump. *Some of fire fighting is well orchestrated, some is not.*

We had two more engines and a ladder truck in different locations with multiple hoses going to the fire. The one from our pumper went to the back of the building where we were alone. We did the best we could with what the two of us had.

While we were PLAYING (*a term we use instead of saying 'squirting' - it sounds more professional*) water on the blaze, one of the firemen came around back and told us that they had taken two of the firefighters to the hospital. This bothered us but we still had a fire to put out.

It wasn't too long before the lieutenant came back to us and told us that one of the two had died and the other was in critical condition. We stopped fighting the fire and got on our knees to say a prayer for the one to recover and for the other one's family.

The fireman who died was a Christian and a good one at that. He was off-duty, driving downtown past his brother-in-law's store, when he saw the flames.

He called the fire department and waited for them to arrive. On their arrival he had taken one of the hand lines to the front of the building, joining another fireman to make entry. Suddenly the front of the building tumbled down onto these two.

The building was a brick building with a wooden roof. When the roof collapsed, the side and front went also. We had a hard time continuing to extinguish the blaze after getting this news.

Fire House Antics

It was early the next morning when I was finally relieved by the oncoming shift.

Remember I had my church-going clothes on? Well, I also had on a new pair of western boots. They were both soaked, and so was I, but I kept the boots on till they dried. That was the only pair of shoes that ever really fit. They shrunk to my feet as they dried.

There were many times the off-duty firemen would hear about a working fire (generally a large one) and come by the station, put on their turnout gear and go to the fire, to work all night or all day without getting a cent more pay or even a day off. They didn't even ask for it. We were firefighters and that is what we did - for pay or not.

Someone told me one time that firefighters must not be too smart and I asked why. He said that people run from a fire but a firefighter will always run to it. Guess it has to be in our blood. Even today I would sooner fight a fire than eat supper. I just love it.

There is a story that the three wise men that attended Jesus were firefighters. Why, we Southerners know the Bible says so. It says they came from "a far".

Charles L. Bose

Fire House Antics

Heater Fire

We had many calls to kerosene heaters in my early days. The homes at that time nearly all had kerosene heat. Most often the heater was placed in the hallways as that was usually the center of the home and it would heat the house nicely. When the first cool weather came along the people would start the heater.

Now to start a kerosene heater, you first turned on the carburetor to start the kerosene flowing - I mean, dripping. That took some time, so families would go and start breakfast while waiting. With the stove on to cook breakfast the kitchen could warm up and the people would forget about the heater.

Later in the morning, the wife would suddenly think about the heater and go light it. By this time there was a puddle of fuel in the heater. The more it burned the hotter it got and the fuel kept coming until the stove would start to breath, sounding like "woof, woof" and the chimney pipe got red hot. When this happened, people panicked. It was so hot that they were afraid to get near it and we were called.

When we got there, there were two things to do to douse the fire. You could turn off the fuel and let it burn out OR put a tray of ice cubes in the furnace and that would cool it and then the flame would subside. If you put water from the fire hose on it, with the pressure it carried, the stove would explode.

One morning we were called to a house and a lady met me at the door, wide-eyed and scared to death. She said the heater was going to burn the house down. I asked her for a tray of ice cubes and she looked at me like I was insane. I'm not sure if she thought that I was hot and wanted to cool off or just what she thought.

I asked her again for a tray of ice. She asked me this time what I was going to do with it. I told her to hurry and get the ice tray and I would show her. She promptly brought the tray of ice.

I opened the furnace door and started throwing the cubes in one at a time. Immediately the fire subsided. She then looked at me in amazement and asked, "Why did it go out?" So then I told her the story of the FIRE TRIANGLE.

The FIRE TRIANGLE … each leg represents heat, fuel or oxygen. If any one of these three elements is removed there cannot be a fire. It takes all three elements to have fire.

In this case the ice cubes cooled the fuel, melted and made steam which removed the oxygen causing the fire to go out. After this all we had to do was turn off the flow of fuel.

Please note: I do not recommend anybody doing this unless you are a trained firefighter. Someone, not observant of conditions around them, can be badly burned.

Fortunately we do not have many kerosene heater fires anymore. Most of the heaters have been replaced. The newer types are better made, more energy efficient, and cheaper to operate.

The Fire Triangle

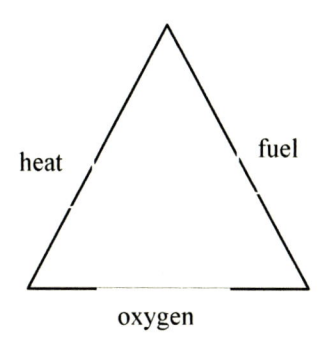

```
       /\
      /  \
heat /    \ fuel
    /      \
   /_____\
     oxygen
```

Charles L. Bose

Afraid to Go Home

Let me tell you about the night I tried to call home. I always stayed up late at night in order to call home before I went to bed. All the other guys called their wives earlier, but at our house my wife always had to help our children do homework, practice the piano, etc. In general she was a busy person, but by eleven o'clock she was usually done and getting ready for bed. I'd call her and talk for a few minutes, then say goodnight.

This night I called and the phone rang and rang. This puzzled me, but I thought she was probably in the shower and couldn't hear the phone ring. So I waited a while, watched some more TV and called again. Again it rang and rang.

I couldn't understand her not answering the phone. She knew I called every night at this time. Oh, well. She's doing some sewing and cannot hear the phone ring. More TV and now some worrying. I try again and the phone rings and rings.

It is now past one o'clock. I begin to wonder what has happened to her. Was she kidnapped? What in the world has happened to her? I don't want to wake my lieutenant. What can I do?

I watched more TV, did more worrying. Funny, when you get into a position like this, what the mind can contrive as possible problems. I had time to contemplate most of them. Finally I woke my lieutenant and told him I had to go home and see what happened to my wife. He agreed with me that I should go home and find out.

Charles L. Bose

I live nine blocks from the fire station, so I drove the department pickup to my house. Those nine blocks seemed like nine miles. As I drove up to the house I didn't see any lights on inside. The door was locked. Everything looked okay to me from the outside.

I've got to go inside! I unlocked the door and eased through the house without turning on lights, stepping as quietly as I could so as not to scare anybody if they were in the house.

Finding nobody downstairs I started upstairs, not wanting to face the prospect of no one being home. I took a deep breath and climbed the stairs to the second floor. It was then that I saw light coming from our bedroom. A little bolder now than before, I charged into the bedroom to find my wife lying in bed with her book in hand sound, and I do mean 'sound', asleep.

I turned the light off, stole down the steps and out of the house and back to the station. I went to bed and had a wonderful night's sleep. The next morning when I returned home I told her what happened.

She apologized and gave me a hug.

Soaked Police

During the early years of my career the required fire fighting protection for daytime was a helmet and a long DAY COAT and at night it included boots, a short coat, pants and helmet. We did not have a SCOTT PACK in that day.

A SCOTT PACK is what we carry on our backs. It is a tank of fresh air that lasts for approximately 30 minutes of normal breathing. When I started as a fireman, we went into smoky buildings without any protection. We got close to the floor and crawled around like a snake. When we came out our lungs, as well as our noses, gave up a black mess. I'm sure you know what I mean. That is why many firefighters developed emphysema and lung diseases.

A lot of times during a fire the police would be there and generally be in our way. We had a special way of dealing with this situation. We didn't have to invite them into the burning building. They seemed to think they were needed and were there anyway.

When we would see one of them nosing around we would act as though we saw fire and make sure the officer got wet. This practice was like a game with us. Sometimes during a fire we had fun, dousing the fire, each other, as well as the police.

During a fire the fire department has total control of the block where the fire is located. The police do not have jurisdiction until we are finished and turn it over to them.

One time we had a fire downtown and we parked the engines along the curb. As we did, a police car pulled in behind us. I had

Charles L. Bose

begun to pull one of the pre-connects just as this happened. I told the officer he could stay there if he was ready to stay till we were finished. When he asked why, I told him I would run my hose through the windows of his car. He found another parking place.

Marina Madness

The department used to have a vehicle called a QUICK ATTACK truck. It was a Suburban with a large dry chemical fire extinguisher and some other small pieces of equipment used for fire suppression.

With this smaller truck we were to patrol the city sixteen hours a day every day; we rode it four hours at a time; there were always two of us in it at a time. In case of a fire there was a good chance we would be on the scene before the engine arrived.

This program afforded us a lot of time to drive all over the city and keep up with its growth; keep us sharp on the streets and hydrant memorization; and get around easier than with the much larger engines.

The concept was good and I'm not sure why it was abandoned, except probably because of added fuel cost. Anyway during this time it got rather boring just driving around town, so we would look for things of interest to do: visit all the swimming pools in the apartment complexes, go to the shopping center, visit the auto train terminal and watch the people. We also spent a lot of time at the city boat ramp.

Sunday around five to six o'clock was the best time to visit the boat ramp. That's when all the boaters were coming back from up the St. Johns River. It was a comedy to watch them; usually they were sunburned, rather inebriated and in a hurry.

Now you add all these ingredients together and a comedy act generally is the result. The scenario goes like this: husband and wife return to the ramp along with many others. They are VERY burnt from the sun reflecting off the water, have had too much to drink and are not happy being in a waiting line to come ashore. When it finally becomes their turn, the man usually gets out of the boat and holds it while his wife goes for the car and boat trailer.

Now everybody knows that the husband is the only one who can back a trailer! But he's giving her directions and she reads or sees them wrong. This starts an argument and the husband exchanges places with the wife saying he can back the trailer and she can watch.

He does back it into the water so the wife can float the boat onto the trailer. He gets out to help, forgets to set the emergency brake and the car backs into the water as they stand there watching.

There are other incidents caused by an excess of drink, people falling out of the boat into the water, etc. The afternoon we spent watching we usually went back to the station and had a good second laugh with the rest of the shift.

Fire House Antics

Charles L. Bose

Airplane Landing

I guess one of the funniest calls I went on was to an airplane on a roof!

The call came in saying an airplane crash-landed on a building south of the station. The building was in line with the flight path at the airport.

Seems an airplane had taken off from Deland Airport and not much after (it's only 25 miles by land to Deland) the pilot discovered he was running out of gas.

He called Sanford Airport requesting emergency landing which was granted. But he had even less gasoline than he thought. The result was that he landed on the roof of an abandoned building.

When we got there, there was no fire, but the engine had come apart from the fuselage. The plane was now abandoned and nobody (*pilot*) was around.

We secured the area and stayed around till the police department came and took charge of the scene. I never knew where the pilot went. Guess I wouldn't want to show my face either, had that happened to me.

Charles L. Bose

Fire House Antics

Car Parks in Marina

We had a call one night about ten o'clock to the lakefront. A car was driven down Palmetto Avenue across Seminole Blvd. and into Lake Monroe, among the boats in the marina.

This is a large marina in this area; the water was approximately 10 feet deep and the lake also has alligators in it.

Anyway, a woman had driven her car into the lake and we were called by the city police to assist in rescue.

In the short time it took us to get to the lake the woman had exited the car and was swimming to one of the boat docks. Three of us shed our turnout gear down to our undershorts and dove into the water.

One of the men swam to the woman and assisted her to the dock; my partner and I swam to the car to help keep its location for removal by a salvage and recovery truck.

As we were sitting on the roof of a car my partner looked at me and said, "You know there are gators in this lake."

"Yep. Just keep on splashing water and they will stay away ... I hope."

We had no trouble with them (gators) but the recovery truck sure had trouble getting the car up and over the sea wall.

The water was very low at the time which made the sea wall from the water to the ground level approximately ten feet. The car was not in the best of shape by the time it reached the street.

This was the first effort of our water rescue team. It had been a struggle to get the team. We had to prove to the city commission that it was really needed. It wasn't easy, but we have a first-class team now.

Stuck Kitten

We were sitting around one day (*which was not unusual*) when I looked out front and saw a car come screeching to a stop across the street. The doors flew open and two young people jumped out. They looked scared to death.

I watched as I got up and walked to the front of the station wondering what was going on. They opened the trunk and pulled out a car wheel. There was no tire on it, but there was a cat halfway through the center hole. I kept watching, as the kids came running into the station.

The two ran up to me and asked, "Can you get the kitten out of the hole?"

I told them I would try. I took the wheel with cat to the rear of the station where we had a shop.

The kids had smeared the wheel and cat with copious amounts of lard. I could hardly hold on to either wheel or cat. The cat's whole upper body was through the hole and stuck around its middle. I took one of its front legs and, as gently as I could, pushed it back through the hole, then took hold of its rear and front parts and pulled till it stretched out and came out of the hole.

The kids were ecstatic; they thought they had lost their kitten.

Charles L. Bose

Fire House Antics

Baby Delivery

There was a call we got ... *keep in mind that most of our calls were not funny but very serious, often life threatening* ... but this one was funny.

A woman who was a friend of my family was pregnant. We took her daughter to our church so we knew her fairly well. We saw her here and there, at the grocery store and when we picked up her child to go to church.

I was on duty when we got a call to her address. I recognized it right away; the call reported that there was a baby to deliver.

As always, the ambulance was called. This was before we transported and all patient transporting was done by a private ambulance. We responded to the address and were met at the door by her husband.

We went to the room where she was and told her we would have to make a preliminary exam so we could report it to the ambulance. She emphatically stated that nobody was going to examine her, just take her to the hospital!

The ambulance was taking much longer to get there than I liked. I didn't have a hankering to deliver a baby. I called the ambulance company and asked what their 10-20 (*location*) and their ETA (*estimated time of arrival*) was. They said, "5 (*minutes*)."

I asked if they could make it sooner. The answer was affirmative. Whew! I then went back to the patient and told her the ambulance was coming. I asked my partner what he thought. He said he couldn't tell anything unless he could examine her. "All she does is cross her legs and say nobody is going to check her except a doctor."

"Where is that ambulance?" I asked myself. I called on the radio again and they said they were on scene. I immediately went outside to meet them, give them the details and help with the gurney.

When we entered the house the paramedic said he was going to have to check for crowning.

Again she said, "NO!" and kept her legs crossed.

She demanded that we take her to the hospital. We loaded her on the gurney and into the ambulance and away we went 10-8 (*lights and siren*) to the hospital.

During the trip the paramedic tried again to make an examination but again she refused.

When we arrived at the hospital and unloaded her, we were met by hospital personnel and they took her in. As the patient was being wheeled down the hallway she delivered her baby.

Fire House Antics

Children and Matches

Being a fire fighter was probably one of the most rewarding times of my life. I guess it's because I just love to be able to help people and be a part of their lives.

I often see people whom I had the privilege of helping at one time or another. I think they also enjoy seeing me and talking a few minutes.

This brings to my mind another incident to share.

I keep worrying about the amount of content of this book and the more I write the more I remember to write. I have thought I was at a closing several times.

Here goes again.

We had a call to a residence. As we approached the house, there was smoke coming out the front door. I told the engineer to charge the proper pre-connect line. *A PRE-CONNECT LINE is usually a 1 ½" cotton jacket hose that is already pre-connected to the pump. All the engineer has to do is set the pump in gear, pull the proper pre-connect lever and the firemen have water.*

Now before he charged the line (hose) I had pulled one hundred and fifty feet of line from the engine, then run back to the fire.

If I did not get all the hose off the truck and the engineer charged it, it would look like a plate of spaghetti. I wouldn't have any water because of the kinks in the hose. It was important for me to pull all the hose from the truck.

Charles L. Bose

As I approached the house I saw people I recognized, but I didn't stop. I went into the house and followed the smoke to a bedroom. The bed was burning but there was not much more damage so I extinguished the fire and returned to the engine to get the SMOKE EJECTOR, nothing more than a large fan that will remove the smoke from the house.

If we don't remove the smoke from the house, it makes it very difficult for the fireman to do the salvage and overhaul. We try as hard as we can to do the least amount of damage. The fire has already caused enough.

As I went back outside I heard my name called by one of the onlookers. It was a teacher whom I knew from the school system. She asked me what caused the fire.

I told her that I found a pack of matches under the bed. *It so happened that this lady was the owner of the house and it was one of her sons who had been playing with the matches.*

She asked me what she should do to him. I told her, "Nothing. He probably has been punished enough already."

She thanked me and assured me she would not spank him.

This young man is now grown up and a parent himself. I hope he remembers to teach his children about fires and safety.

Cat up a Tree

We had a doctor in Sanford who had a home in the fashionable part of town. He also had twelve children. We got a call one day for a cat in a tree in his neighborhood.

This was not an emergency run so we (*the lieutenant and I*) took the brush truck. Remember, the brush truck was a converted old military Dodge power wagon. We had equipped it with a pump and rack for ladders and some brush firefighting equipment.

The day was kind of damp and rainy, and I had not been in the department long and was not used to climbing ladders with boots and coat. When we got to the neighborhood the doctor's wife met us and showed us the tree where the cat was.

It was in the very top of a palm tree that had had its top cut out. The cat was in the tree, sitting where the top had been, approximately 40 feet up from the ground.

The lieutenant and I got an extension ladder off the truck and set it up against the tree. I looked at him and he at me. Then he said, "Climb up and get the cat."

Now I'm not stupid. I know what happens when you grab a scared cat and I wasn't ready for any first aid on me. I made a feeble attempt to climb the ladder, when the lieutenant said, "Let me do it."

I graciously allowed him.

When he reached the top of the tree he grabbed the cat by the nape of the neck and held it over the side. "Can you catch him?"

"Sure", I replied.

Charles L. Bose

Now get this picture: me at the base of the ladder and my lieutenant forty feet up a tree with a scared cat in his hand. Now **add** to this picture twelve children all in a line *with Mama* watching.

The lieutenant turned the cat loose and down it came. As it came closer, almost in slow motion it spread all fours; its claws seemed to be an inch long and its teeth like fangs.

Like I said, I'm not stupid. As the cat came close I decided I couldn't catch it and so ….

When the cat hit the ground I looked at the mother and apologized for not being able to catch the cat. She said she didn't blame me. She would not have done it either.

The cat hit the ground and was stunned for a couple seconds and then took off running. All the kids thought the cat was dead 'til it ran off, then they ran off too.

We retrieved the ladder, put it back on the truck and went back to the station.

We quit "rescuing" cats in trees when we couldn't find any cat bones in trees. They always come down when they get hungry.

Lost Child

Many of the incidents that happened when I was an active firefighter were amusing and a lot of fun. Most fires, I say most **fires**, were fun. You can replace things but not lives, so, as long as there was no life lost, fighting a fire was like a game to me. Challenge: Could I put it out or would it burn down?

I've thought of another incident that was by no means a happy one. It involved the life of a child. To loose a child impacted the whole department.

This particular incident happened during a severe rainstorm. It happened in one of the housing projects here in town. There was and still is a drainage ditch that runs through the project and a small walk bridge is used to get across the ditch.

The ditch was running full and sometimes overflowing. Children were out playing around and one of them fell in. By the time we got the call and arrived on the scene there were so many stories as to where he fell in that we didn't know where to start or with what. So we all took off our shoes and waded in.

We used ropes tied to us to keep us safe from the strong current. We felt with our hands and feet both up and down the bank, through the culvert, under the road and all the way to Lake Monroe, which would have been almost a mile.

Searching through the normal amount of trash accumulation for that distance would be bad enough but the raging current picked up even more, making our job nearly impossible. We searched for several days finding nothing. The water was muddy but we kept on looking in every direction, studying the location for possible areas of entrapment.

We had every idea the body was entrapped, but where? We did not know. We kept on looking all day and late into the evening. The next day the same thing. Many off-duty firemen came in to help. We had the city's heavy equipment on scene but agreed not to use it for fear of damage to the body if found.

As the water began to subside we were more able to see what we were doing. The ditch went under the road and then took a hard right turn. This is the area we suspected held the body. It was not until the water subsided greatly that we were able to get into the tangle of brush, tree limbs, etc. and sure enough, the body had become entangled in the brush pile. It was a sad sight, but, oddly enough, a sense of relief filled us that we were able to find the little fellow.

It makes you mad when a child's life is lost by drowning in a swimming pool or, in this case, by parental neglect.

Fire House Antics

Charles L. Bose

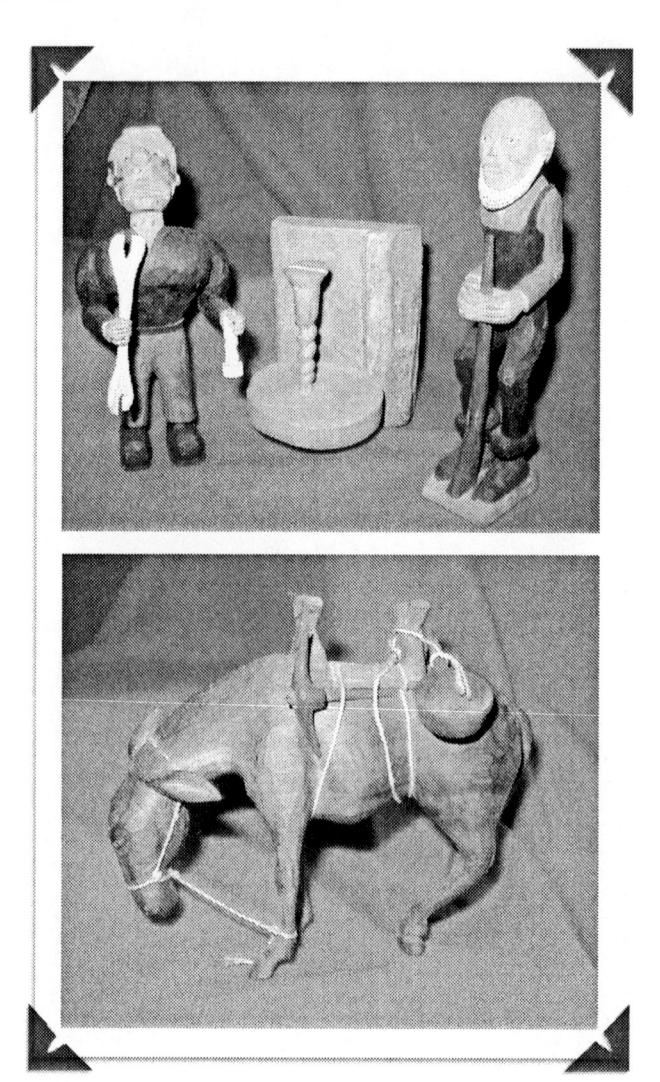

Fire House Antics

Spare Time Activities

When I was hired by the City of Sanford Fire Department there were requirements that I had to meet. In other words, we were on probation and it lasted for one year. We had to prove ourselves worthy of the name Fireman.

We had to learn how to drive the engines, learn all the streets and hydrants, know all the ten codes for radio transmissions, know hydraulics, friction loss, pump pressure, nozzle pressure, proper use of all types of ladders, and be able to raise an extension ladder.

We also had to know how to use the water that we carried on board the engines to the best advantage. We carried 500 gallons of water on each truck. We used that water first. We didn't like to hook to a hydrant, because that meant a lot more work.

When we returned to the station we had to wash the hose. It was usually muddy from the water that leaked from the hose couplings and made the ground muddy. After washing the hose we had to FLAKE it in the sun to dry.

FLAKING A HOSE *means to rest the flattened hose on its side and set it in a zig-zag shape so as much of the hose surface as possible is able to dry.*

The outer jacket of the hose is made of cotton. If we were to pack it back on the truck when it was still wet, the hose would mildew, allowing a weakness to develop in the hose. While that damp hose dried, we packed the engine with spare dry hose from racks in the station.

Charles L. Bose

After we passed probation we were declared a city fireman, and we were protected by the city civil service board.

Most of our training took place during the day. We learned how to fight different types of fires and we practiced driving the trucks and setting up the pumps. We were busy most of the day perfecting our trade. The better we got the less chance we had of getting hurt later. Our evenings and weekends were ours to do as we pleased, but we had to remain ready.

During the hours that were ours some of the men chose to do many different things. One man took up knife making and gun repair, which made him a few more dollars. Retired now, he does it full time to supplement his retirement income.

I had been interested in wood since I was a child. As a Boy Scout I did some carving for a merit badge, so with some time on my hands I went back to carving.

I remember one Saturday or Sunday at #2 Station, while I was carving what was suppose to be a mule, another fireman was sitting at the kitchen table watching me. He was a rancher when he was off duty. He had a couple hundred head of beef cows.

On occasion I would help him round up his cows to count and brand them. We had to ride horseback down in the Florida swamp to chase them out. It was cool down there and the cows liked that.

As we sat there at the table he finally asked me what I was carving. I told him it was a mule, "Can't you see?"

"No" was his answer. "It looks more like a horse to me and I should know what a horse looks like."

Fire House Antics

He told me he couldn't whittle but if I'd listen to him, he would tell me what a mule looked like and I could carve it to look like one.

We sat at that table for many an hour; he'd tell me what to do and I'd do it. The piece of wood kept taking more shape 'til it did look like a mule.

I have also carved a ball in a cage with a chain attached, and many figures, including several birds and pairs of wooden pliers. Later, when the State of Florida started community colleges, many of the newer firemen started going to college to get a degree in fire science. Their spare time is now taken with studying.

Charles L. Bose

Helplessness

Dr. Smith was a physician here in Sanford, loved by everybody. He is the same doctor I wrote about who had twelve children and their cat was in a forty-foot palm tree.

One day we received a call "person down". We knew the address and the people who lived there. The doctor and his family were long time Sanford residents.

As we left the station we wondered aloud about what could be so wrong that the doctor couldn't take care it. We were wondering what to expect all the way to the address.

As we gathered our medical paraphernalia and O_2, we heard a male voice from the front door pleading, "Hurry up! My wife is not breathing."

Now we knew what to expect and what we had to do. We entered the house and were told by the doctor that his wife was lying on the floor in the kitchen.

I have felt sorry for people many times, but my heart just broke for this man. There he stood with a M. D. degree, a stethoscope around his neck and was not able to treat his own wife.

We immediately started CPR. The doctor asked us to holler her name. *Many times, when a person is unconscious and you call their name, they will respond.* So we hollered "Peg" to her many times, but to no avail. We kept performing CPR and administering O_2 'til the ambulance arrived. One of us who was performing CPR rode in the ambulance to the hospital continuing to do CPR.

Charles L. Bose

When we arrived at the hospital she was taken to the emergency room where the staff doctor did everything he could, but she did not survive.

Fire House Antics

Post Office Fire

I went on vacation one year to my mom and dad's home in Ohio, where I was born and raised in a town called Beach City. The town of Beach City didn't have a clue what a beach was. It is approximately sixty miles from Lake Erie. No where near a beach. It was the founder of the town whose name was Beach.

I was talking to Mom and Dad, when I heard the fire siren. There is a siren in the business district of Beach City that is blown each day at noon. It was used as an air raid siren during the war; now it is the fire siren to call the volunteer firemen to the station.

Being a volunteer department the first volunteer to get to the station gets to drive the engine. Driving the truck is a big thing for a volunteer to do because he can drive fast and not get caught by the police. I never got that much of a rush driving the truck; I always got more pleasure manning the hose.

When I heard the siren I went out the front door of the house to see which way the trucks went. As I watched I figured I might as well go to the Station and find out where the fire was.

I told my wife I was going to the station to see what was going on. She later told me that my mom said to her, "Charles (*that's what she called me*) will not go into the fire if there is one."

My wife told Mom, "You don't know Chuck as well as I thought you did. He'll be in the middle of it if he has his way."

My wife was right.

Charles L. Bose

The fire was in the post office in a neighboring town. The flames were really showing by the time I got there and the trucks from my town arrived. I saw the volunteer fire chief from that town; I introduced myself to him and ask if I could help. I told him I was a fireman from Florida, and I was on vacation. He said he would be glad for me to help.

I told him that we needed to make entry into the building. He said it was a government building and we couldn't go in unless we asked the Postmaster to unlock it and let us in.

This puzzled me, so I ask if we were just going to let the building burn down because the Postmaster wasn't there to let us in.

He replied, "I guess so."

I agreed it was a government building but told him that was no reason for us not to make entry. He agreed and we breached the door and made entry with hoses in hand and lots of water.

It didn't take very much to bring the fire under control. Then there was another problem.

There was mail scattered all over the floor, some wet and all of it tramped on. I asked the Chief what we were going to do with all the mail. To this he replied that we would wait 'til the Postmaster got there and he could do with it whatever he wanted.

By this time I was convinced that the name "Chief" was only an empty title that this man wore, so I suggested that we gather all the mail together and put it under lock and key. It was, after all, government property.

Fire House Antics

He asked me where we could find a place to secure it. I suggested that since the city had a jail with cells, why not put it all in a cell and have the police lock it up. And that is what they did.

I went back, bedraggled and tired, to Mom's place after the fire was extinguished.

My mom, bless her heart, asked me what I had been doing.

My response? "Fighting a fire."

My wife's remark? "I told you."

Fighting a fire for an hour or two is about the same as working a normal job for eight hours - a person is absolutely exhausted. We put every ounce of energy into the time it takes to put the fire out. When the fire is finally out we nearly collapse.

A fire does not have to be in your hometown to fight. I'll fight any fire; it doesn't matter where it is. That is the reason that firefighters from the East and South East go to the West to fight forest fires. I know a firefighter from Brasstown, N.C. who came down here and fought the forest fire we had several years ago.

Charles L. Bose

Coon under Hood

I have not written anything about the car fires we had, but I told you about medical emergencies and other types of fires. A car fire is attacked much the same way as a house or industrial fire. It is attacked with a lot of caution, most especially if the fire is under the hood or in the trunk. These two places are more dangerous because of the presence of gasoline.

FYI: Because of the new type of hood and trunk latch device, so many times, if there is a fire in the hood or trunk compartment, they are difficult to open without doing a lot of body damage to the hood or trunk. The cable that is used to open the hood and trunk will melt in half leaving the latch inoperable, so firemen have to pry them open.

We had a call to a car fire downtown in a residential area. On our arrival there appeared to be large quantities of smoke coming from under the hood.

The owner told us she had just driven to town and back, which was only ten blocks, and when she parked the car all this smoke came from under the hood.

As I said before, we always approach a car fire with caution; this car was no exception. As I released the hood latch I had one of my firemen standing by with a booster line so he could apply water as soon as the hood was opened. But as soon as I opened the hood it became clear to us that the smoke was not smoke but rather steam. *Steam and smoke are white but steam is much hotter and damper.*

We also saw where the steam was coming from. One of the heater hoses had ruptured and the insulation under the hood was shredded.

My mind raced to figure out what had happened to this car when my eyes fell upon the largest raccoon I have ever seen. He had, apparently, climbed into the engine compartment to stay warm the night before. *As I remember, it was cool that day.*

When the owner of the car started the engine to go to town, I imagine that raccoon got hit a couple times on the rear end causing him to get rather mad. He might have even gotten shocked if he'd touched any of the spark plug wires.

This raccoon was not just mad. He was furious!

A police officer is always dispatched to any fire or emergency that we had, and there was an officer with us. When he saw the raccoon, he drew his service revolver and told me he was going to shoot it.

"No, I think I can get it out a better way," I replied.

There was an empty trash can and a large stick near by. I asked one of my firemen to bring them to me. They wondered how I was going to remove the raccoon with a stick. I took the stick and started gently poking him. When he got mad enough to grab the stick between his teeth, I pulled him out, dumped him in the trash can and put on the lid.

One of the firemen suggested we take him to the zoo. We all agreed and there we went. The zoo keeper met us, puzzled by the

Fire House Antics

arrival of the fire department. We told her we had a new resident for her.

When we dumped Mr. Coon in with the rest of the raccoons, they sensed that this one was angry. As he walked toward the rest of them they all just spread apart like the Red Sea was spread for the Israelites and our Mr. Coon took charge.

Charles L. Bose

Fire House Antics

Determined to Burn

When I started working at the Fire Department we were not allowed to fight a fire outside of the city limits unless a piece of city equipment was involved. I think I've mentioned this before.

We had a call one day to the Post Office, "a car on fire". Upon our arrival there was smoke coming from the passenger compartment. This indicated that the fire was either electrical or that the seats were on fire. The owner was standing there watching us and the car; he told us that the seat was on fire.

We opened the door and extinguished the fire. It was not a policy but more of a courtesy to examine the condition of the auto and determine the extent of damage. We determined that his car could be driven home and told the owner as much.

"Take it home and have the seats repaired."

He seemed to take our advice and drove away. We went back to the station.

Later that same day we got another call to a car fire on a street that was half in and half out of the city limits. As we approached the car we saw that it was outside the city limits. We also noticed that it was the same car that we had extinguished earlier that day at the Post Office.

There was nobody near the car and we were not allowed to extinguish it, so we left it and went back to the station.

I'm sure the owner had a reason to want the car to burn; probably for the insurance. He got his wish, I guess.

Charles L. Bose

Let me explain why we were not allowed to fight a fire outside the city limits. The people of the city paid city taxes which paid our wages. The county residents paid only county taxes.

Today there is a county fire department. And there is a mutual agreement between the cities and the county to fight all fires regardless of location.

Muck Fire

Still another type of fire we have to battle here in Florida is the muck or peat moss fires. I said a battle because a battle it is. It's not as dangerous as a structure fire but still the chance to get hurt presents itself, just in a different way. In a structure fire we are more concerned about the ceiling or roof caving in on us.

We also had the electrical and chemical hazard to deal with, but with a muck fire you could very easily break your leg and, worse yet, fall into one of the burning pockets. Structure fires are generally over in a couple hours, but a muck fire can and usually does burn on for days.

Muck fires burn underground forming pockets of ash and embers. These pockets can get to be very large in size. The most dangerous thing with this type fire is that you cannot see flames. You can see where it has burned, because the top soil will cave in after the fire has consumed all the muck.

If the fire were all in one spot it would be easy to fight, but it is not. The fire travels.

The way we fought a muck fire was to take a one and a half inch hose and attach a six foot piece of ½ inch pipe to it, pick a spot and poke the pipe into the ground with water flowing. When you found a hole, the pipe would nearly drop out of sight and a lot of ash would come out of the ground like a volcano. You would keep moving doing the same thing till you established a perimeter.

Charles L. Bose

Once a perimeter was established, we would hook up our 2 ½" line to a hydrant and flood the area. We continued using the pipe probe to make sure the perimeter did not move. *Some of these fires burn for a week.* Every day at least one fireman spent the day at the muck fire.

All of the muck fires were in the summer when it was dry and the muck would burn easily. The fires were started probably by people burning trash or discarding a lighted cigarette.

Jail Fire

This fire was probably one of the most tragic fires I ever fought or witnessed during my employment on the fire department. The fire and loss of life were unnecessary.

The county jail lacked a lot of things that were later mandated by order of state or federal government, but this fire didn't happen because of poor conditions. This happened because one inmate somehow had a pack of matches.

Near his cell was a stack of mattresses. *They were replacing the mattresses with the fire retardant type.* The inmate with the matches struck one of the matches and threw it on the mattress stack, causing it to ignite. *A burning mattress will put off some of the most toxic smoke to be found, due to the foam rubber inside them.*

As I remember, I was off duty that day, working at the fire equipment company that I owned. The business was located downtown about five or six blocks from the jail. I remember hearing the fire sirens coming toward town and wondering where they were going.

I stepped outside to take a look and to see if I saw smoke. Sure enough, smoke was coming from the area of the county court house. I knew that if there was smoke from that area I would be needed. I drove, following the smoke to the county jail.

There was smoke coming from every crack in the building. I immediately went to the front door where I was allowed to enter.

Charles L. Bose

Everybody there knew all the firemen. As I entered the building there was so much smoke that you could hardly see, let alone breathe.

From the time fire was discovered 'til I got there, cell blocks were being opened. There was no way for us to make any kind of neat rescue. We just went into the cells, took the inmates by the arms and dragged them out to a staging area where they were either taken to the hospital or pronounced dead.

The county jail at that time was attached to the county courthouse. We had to evacuate the courthouse as well.

Many perished unnecessarily that day, including the one who set the fire.

The Fire Fighter

(I wrote this song dedicated to the City of New York Fire Department)

My sleep is short with that deafening alarm.
In less than three minutes, I'm dressed and gone.
We charge through the night in spite of the unknown
The fire is blazing hot as brimstone.

I am a firefighter, my passion is alive.
I give myself, so others survive.
My companions and I are a tight brotherhood.
They become my family and my livelihood.
I get a lot of contentment and a little pay.
It's not the money that makes me want to stay.

When it's beyond my means, I break down and weep
If I lose a life, I cannot eat, I cannot sleep
But I must go on, other lives to save.
This emotional man must continue to be brave.

With air pack on my back I run up the stairs
Exhausted I climb I leap them in pairs
Lungs bursting for air in the smoke and the rubble
Up and up I climb to rescue those in trouble
The sweat stings my eyes, even with a mask I choke
This inferno tortures me mid the blaze and the smoke

Charles L. Bose

Though bunker gear I wear I feel the heat therein
The flames overlap me - heat without heat within

Now here's my tribute to the New York's fallen sons
You have given your all your job now done
You now rest in peace no more smoke or sorrow
No more sweat or fear, you have entered your tomorrow
Because you loved people, you did your job, gave your life
Your final alarm sounded, no more peril no strife.

Copyright Oct, 2001
Sandy Meloon & Firefighter Chuck Bose

Conclusion

I hope I have not bored you with my memories and I hope you had a couple good laughs, possibly some tears.

I had a lot of tears recalling some of the incidents; some were tears of laughter, some tears of sorrow, but that is life.

Thanks for reading **Firehouse Antics**

Charles L. Bose

Acknowledgements

Many thanks …

to Pat Fosselius, for her eagerness to type the pages of this book taken from my hand-written pages;

to the City of Sanford for allowing me to give them 25 years of my life to a job I loved and still do;

to my many brothers acquired from different fire departments;

and especially to Kace for the graphics work and editing.

Charles L. Bose

Glossary of terms

10-20: what is your location?

10-98-10-19: Fire is out and returning to station

Booster Line: 1" rubber coated hose

Day coat: a long coat used during daylight hours

Night coat: a shorter version of the day coat but used with pants and boots

Turnout gear: helmet, boots, day coat or night coat

Engine: a fire truck

Line: fire hose

Pre-connect: a fire hose pre-connected to the pump

Scott pack or MSA (all the same but from different manufacturers): self-contained breathing apparatus

To set up truck: to engage pump and regulate proper pressure at nozzle

Charles L. Bose

Comparisons

Here are some comparisons that you might be interested in. It shows how our fire department has grown over more than one hundred years.

The comparisons I will be using are ones that were told to me by one of my retired chiefs. Some of these comparisons are with data when I was hired.

The calls:

In 1964 we had approximately 300 fire calls per year in a city of about 17,000 population. We did not run EMS until later.

In 1973 that number jumped to approximately 600 calls per year.

In 2003 they are running 10,000 per year and Sanford's population is approximately 40,000. That is quite an increase.

The personnel:

In 1964 we had 25 firefighters including the two Chiefs.

In 1973 we had 35 fire fighters plus the two chiefs and a training officer.

In 2003 there are 70 personnel.

The budget:

The budget in 1978 was $900,000.00

The budget in 2003 is $5,000,000.00

Charles L. Bose

Reviews

This book is filled with details and clever stories. These are not stories of a vivid imagination but actually occurred. I know; I was there. A good testimonial to the past and present Fire Department.

J. Thomas Hickson
SFD Fire Chief (retired)
1973-2003

It's a delight to read! It's as if you're there with Chuck, listening to and reliving an incredible life. He succeeded with the laughter and the tears.

Kace Montgomery

Chucks talent as a storyteller shines through from the funny experiences to the more serious job as a firefighter. This book will inspire all those who read it.

Stephanie Ziegenfuss

Charles L. Bose

About the Author

My name is Charles L. Bose, originally from the Buckeye State of Ohio. I left there to join the U.S. Navy in 1956. I was stationed in Sanford, Florida, for three of my four years in the U. S. Navy. I then went to work as a mechanic, as that is what I knew best.

I was raised in Ohio. My father was a finish carpenter, my mother a nurse. This background surely had a bearing on the direction my life would take. I became an EMT (emergency medical technician) in the Fire Department and I still enjoy medicine. I did not become a paramedic or ever have a desire to do so. I do enjoy what medical knowledge I gained in the department and have had occasion to use it since retirement.

I am also an avid wood worker. I make and play musical instruments: mandolins, guitars, banjos, dulcimers and psalteries, etc.

I am the father of two children, Mark and Alice Margaret, and grandfather to six. I own the home we live in. My wife is a retired schoolteacher. We have lived here in Sanford since 1957.

The city of Sanford, Florida, is on the banks of Lake Monroe. The St. Johns River runs through Lake Monroe on its way to Jacksonville from down Melbourne way. Sanford was one time known as the CELERY CAPITAL OF THE WORLD.

I remember there was this machine that they called the MULE TRAIN. It would go into the celery field with a crew of people, approximately 20. They would pick, grade, trim, box and load the crates onto waiting trucks that would take them to the cooler where later they would be shipped. But I digress.

I came to Sanford in July of 1957, on one of those hot, muggy Florida days. I was being transferred from Memphis, Tennessee to Sanford to serve in the US Navy at the US Naval Air Station. I was an aircraft jet engine mechanic. I served four years in the Navy with a year and a half at sea aboard aircraft carriers.

I worked a couple years as a mechanic in a couple of car dealerships here in Sanford before I got the chance to be a firefighter. I had fire fighting training in the U.S. Navy, but never did I think I would some day be a firefighter.

I later joined the Sanford Fire Department and spent the next 25 years there and retired. I started my career in the fire department at the age of 28 on April 1, 1964. What a day to start a new career, April Fool's Day!!!

During those 25 years I attained an officer rank. Actually it was a Jr. Lieutenant. Most departments have firefighter, engineer, Lieutenant, Battalion Chief, Deputy Chief and Chief. Ours at that time were firefighter, senior firefighter, Lieutenant, Battalion Chief, Assistant Chief and Chief. My rank was Senior Firefighter.

I attended EMT classes but not paramedic. I saw a lot of growth in the fire service like the additions of the EMT, the paramedic and water rescue. I also saw a town grow from a farm community to a thriving city.

There are two things that I never thought I would do; in fact, I never gave it a thought. One was being a firefighter, the other authoring a book.

Printed in the United States
20997LVS00001B/91-129